On the farm the horse was used for almost every type of work. This postcard was obviously specially posed as the oast house is the other way! It shows a typical scene at hop-picking time, and would have found a ready market among the many casual hop-pickers who came from the towns, especially London, for a working holiday in Kent each year. This example is quite small for a farm cart, and more often a four-wheeled cart and a team of horses would be used. (Published by Mockford, Tonbridge, postally used 11th October 1905, Tunbridge Wells to Goudhurst.)

GW00729074

A charming study of bygone harvesting methods, with three horses working a reaper, while the cut corn is arranged in stooks. This is a later view taken at the foot of the North Downs to the west of Snodland. (Published by Hambrook Bros., Snodland, postally used 30th July 1927, Snodland to Bexleyheath.)

Some of the heavy work on the farm was done by traction engines, with special teams moving from farm to farm. They were used for ploughing the heavier soils and to work the threshing machine at harvest time, as in this view at Garlinge Farm, between Margate and Birchington. (Published by W.R. The Saxon Series, a local Thanet firm about 1906.)

1

Although most people are familiar with the double-deck horse-bus found in the larger towns, these horse-drawn brakes were equally common and were popular around the coastal towns, running both local bus services and excursions. In many cases the operators of these vehicles did little to publicise their identity, but in this picture 'G.T. Gladdish, Whitstable.' is clearly displayed on the canopy of the leading brake. The same name appears on the second brake (behind the lamp) in small letters, which is all that is legally required. (This exceptionally sharp photograph, probably of a Sunday School outing, was taken in 1908, but alas the publisher is unknown.)

This is the first of several cards of Birchington Square, probably taken after the Great War. Although motorised transport increased rapidly at this time, horse brakes continued to ply for holiday traffic well into the 'twenties in the Thanet resorts. The coach and four, complete with liveried footman and driver, would have been quite rare by this time. (Published by H. Camburn, Tunbridge Wells, for F. Pointer, Birchington, postally used 3rd September 1920, Birchington to Headcorn.)

The Folkestone, Sandgate and Hythe Tramways Company ran a horse-drawn service between the last two locations, which opened in 1892. From 1894 the line became a subsidiary of the South Eastern Railway, who were looking for an alternative route to Folkestone Harbour. However, these plans never came to fruition, nor did later plans to electrify the line.

Rolling stock consisted of a closed saloon (1), two covered toastracks (2 & 4), and two open toastracks (3 & 5). In this postcard one of the covered cars stands at the Sandgate terminus, while horse cabs in line await customers. (Anon, c1908.)

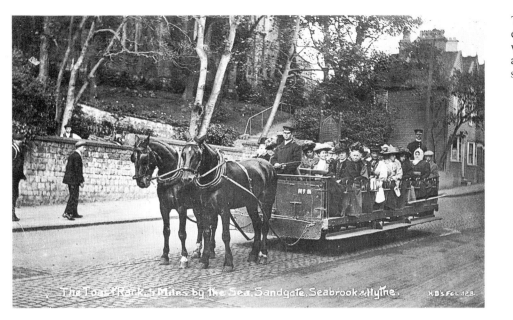

The Toast Rack, 5 Miles by the Sea, Sandgate, Seabrook & Hythe.   H.B's Fol. 123.

The line suffered badly from competition from early charabancs, so it was past its heyday when this postcard was produced of car No. 5 at the Sandgate terminus. (H.B.'s F&L series; sent Folkestone to London, 22nd June 1913.)

The trams did not operate during WWI, and then ran only in the summer until the line closed at the end of September 1921. This view is of a well-loaded open car, also at the Sandgate terminus, towards the end of the tramway's life. Observe the changes between the two views, especially the dress of the passengers. (Anon, sent from Sandgate to Peckham Rye, 15th August 1919.)

The Toast Rack, Sandgate Seabrook, Hythe

Sandgate

3628 B.

A short distance from the horse trams was the lower terminus of the Sandgate Hill Lift Company Ltd line. This opened in 1892 and closed in 1918; it was 670 feet long, rose about 120 feet and worked on the hydraulic counterbalance system. The two tram-like cars seated sixteen passengers. (Peacock Brand, c1903.)

Although one cliff lift survives at Folkestone, a second lift operated from 1904 to 1939 between Lower Sandgate Road and the Leas near the Metropole Hotel. It worked on sea-water pumped from the lower station; observe the flag at the upper station which always flew when the lift was operating. (Published by Cross Library, Folkestone, posted 12th September 1907, Folkestone to Bexleyheath.)

Metropole Lift, Folkestone.

The first electric trams in the area were at Dover. Two routes, to Buckland and Maxton, were opened in 1897 by Dover Corporation Tramways. The initial fleet was ten trams built by Brush of Loughborough and it included No. 9 seen here at the Town Hall stop. (Anon, sent from Dover to Bath, 17th September 1905.)

Another of the 1897 trams crosses the River Dour at Buckland heading towards the town centre. The door of Buckland tram depot can be seen on the far left of the picture. Note how little protection from the elements the driver had on these early trams. (Anon, c1910)

A later Dover tram at the Town Hall; this one is No. 17, which was unique in the fleet. It was built in 1902 by The Electric Railway & Tramway Carriage Works Ltd and was the first tram with the more modern style of bodywork, with the upper deck extended over the platforms. No. 17 carried twenty-six passengers outside and twenty-two inside; it was their only car with reversed stairs, but in 1918 it was rebuilt with normal half-turn stairs to match the rest of the fleet. (Published by the YMCA and sent from N30 General Hospital to Paris; no date, but it is passed by the censor and written in French. It was sent by a wounded American soldier, serving in France, from hospital in Dover during WWI.)

The Isle of Thanet Tramways & Lighting Company Ltd opened its extensive system on 4th April 1901 (between Margate and Ramsgate Harbour via Dumpton) and on 6th July 1901 (the remaining sections to Westbrook, Ramsgate Town Station and via Broadstairs). This view shows tram No. 39 at Margate Harbour passing a row of horse brakes, whose operators complained of lost trade when the trams began. (Published by J. Davis, London, about 1905.)

Margate.   The Marine Parade.

1137

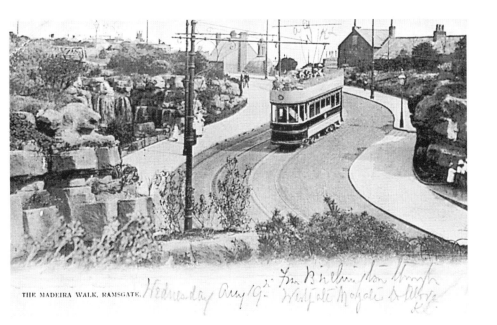

THE MADEIRA WALK, RAMSGATE.

The initial trams were built in America by the St Louis Car Co. and shipped in kit form to Britain. Nos 1-20 were truck-mounted fifty-five seaters and Nos 21-40, mounted on bogies, were four feet longer at 33 feet and sat sixty-eight passengers. All had reversed stairs and enclosed driving positions. Bogie car No. 29 descends the sharply curved Madeira Walk towards Ramsgate Harbour. (No publisher shown, but sent from Ramsgate to Ealing, 12th August 1903.)

5

The bogie cars were prone to derail and also suffered braking problems; following a serious runaway in August 1903 with one of these cars it was decided to convert them to run on trucks that could be fitted with a track brake. As no truck could carry such a long body, they were shortened by some five feet, leaving the saloon with four and a half side windows instead of six. This later postcard shows a rebuilt No. 34 climbing Madeira Walk. (Anon again, sent Ramsgate to London, 28th August 1912.)

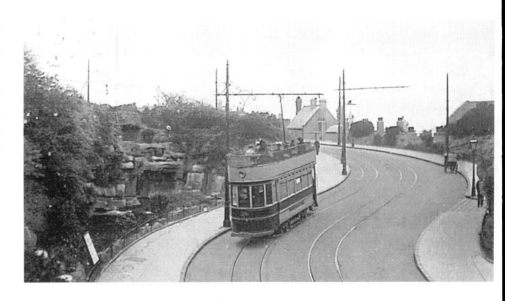

A busy scene at the Ramsgate Harbour terminus with a shortened ex-bogie car No. 27 heading for Ramsgate Town Station, while in the spur is No. 47, one of a batch of ten Milnes cars obtained at short notice in 1901 to strengthen the fleet. They were added to (and were identical to) an order for Chatham & District, and they worked the Ramsgate Harbour to Broadstairs via Gladstone Road service. In this view the conductor is just walking round the trolley, while the pointman, lever in hand, stands ready to work the points. (A Silverette card by Raphael Tuck, London, sent from Margate to Reading on 19th August 1905.)

In 1905 there were two major tram accidents in Ramsgate, further darkening the reputation of the Thanet trams. On 26th May No. 47 (pictured above) ran into a shop, while on 3rd August No. 41 ran out of control descending Madeira Walk in the rain, crashing through the fence and into some waste ground thirty feet below. Luckily there were only six passengers and only the driver was badly hurt. No. 41 was scrapped, but some parts were used to repair No. 47. (Published by Swaine, Broadstairs, and sent from Ramsgate to Redhill seventeen days after the accident.)

The Front, Margate

A busy scene at Margate about 1925 showing both Isle of Thanet trams and buses; nearest the camera is one of four Thornycroft double-deckers from 1919, followed by tram No. 4, while one of the numerous 20-seat Thornycrofts, often used to compete with the small charabancs the small firms used to cream off the profitable summer traffic, passes in the opposite direction. (No publisher.)

Sheerness had the smallest tram system in Kent, with just eight cars. It also had the shortest life, running from 1903 to 1917. Unusually it used bow collectors, rather than trolleys. Also on this card is the former Sheerness-on-Sea station opened in 1883 (the original 1860 station was near the Dockyard) and demolished in February 1971 when a train failed to stop. (Sent from Sheerness to Chatham, 22nd July 1911, no publisher shown.)

Sheerness-on-Sea   High Street

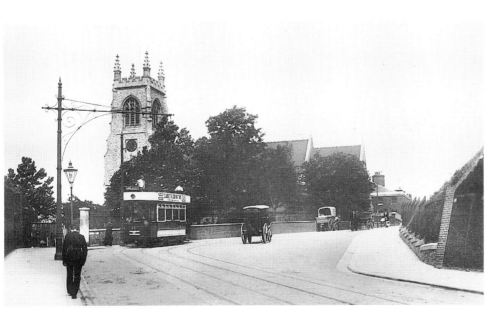

The Chatham & District Light Railway's tram services commenced in June 1902 with routes to Chatham Cemetery, Chatham Dockyard and Gillingham (Victoria Bridge/Pier Road) via Brompton or Jezreels. Later routes reached Rainham, Strood, Borstal and Frindsbury. Leaving Chatham for Gillingham via Brompton is No. 10, one of the original batch of twenty-five built by Milnes of Hadley, Shropshire. They were fitted with fifty-two seats and reversed stairs. (Published by W.H. Smiths, Kingsway Real Photo Series, about 1910.)

The focal point of the C & D lines was outside the grand Chatham Town Hall. No. 17 heads for Victoria Bridge, while on the right a second tram awaits to depart towards Luton Arches. (Published by Valentines, Dundee, and sent from Chatham to Bexhill, 4th January 1913.)

The same view three-quarters of an hour (and about thirty years) later. The trams ceased after 30th September 1930, and were replaced by these Leyland Titan TD1 double-deckers, with fully enclosed 48-seat bodies. Chatham & District continued to run buses until 1955, when they were absorbed by Maidstone & District. (An Excel Series postcard used on 31st August 1938, Chatham to Kelvedon.)

The final extension of the Chatham & District network was the route to Borstal, opened in August 1908. This tranquil view at the Borstal terminus shows No. 24, a 1903 Brush-built car, with its crew and local children posing for the photographer. (Published by G. Banbury, Haywards Heath and sent from Rochester to Littlebourne, 25th May 1923.)

8

Maidstone Corporation's tramway opened in July 1904 from the town centre to Barming. The initial fleet consisted of six open-top cars built by the Electric Railway & Tramway Carriage Company. This postcard shows No. 2, still in 'as new' condition, leaving the first crossing loop from the Barming terminus on its journey into town. (A Young & Cooper, Maidstone, postcard, 1904.)

Car No. 4 at the town centre terminus, by Queen Victoria's Monument. By this time the tram has been festooned with adverts. This is a hand-coloured postcard, and the tram has been coloured green, despite Maidstone's trams being brown! (Valentines, Dundee, was the errant publisher, about 1906.)

Dartford Council Tramways on opening day, 14th February 1906, with decorated trams at the depot in Victoria Road. The main line service ran from Bexley Heath to Horns Cross, with a branch service from Victoria Road to Wilmington. The fleet consisted of twelve United Electric Car trams, later joined by a single-deck car for the Wilmington service. The entire fleet was lost in a depot fire in August 1917, but fortunately the adjoining Bexley UDC trams were able to cover services, especially for munitions workers at Vickers. (No publisher, sent 2nd April 1906, Dartford to East Greenwich.)

28150   Gravesend. St. James' Church.

Gravesend and Northfleet were served by horse-trams from 1883, and during 1889/90 there was an early experiment with electrical conduit traction. The horse-trams ceased in 1901 and the line reopened in August 1902 using overhead electric traction. Subsequent extensions were opened to Swanscombe, Denton and Pelham Road in the same year. Lines along Windmill Street and Dover Road completed the system the following year. Twenty trams were supplied by the Electric Railway & Tramway Carriage Works, Preston, in 1902. Ten were on trucks (Nos. 11-20) and ten were larger bogie cars, like No. 8 shown here on the service from St James' Church to Pelham Arms. The bogie cars proved to be too large for the demand and in 1904/5 they were sold to other systems and replaced by smaller truck-mounted cars. The church, on the junction of Pelham Road and Overcliffe, was demolished in 1968, and a rather unattractive office block is now on the site. (A Photochrom of Tunbridge Wells postcard, no later than 1905.)

Another attempt to reduce costs came in 1904 when two one-man-operated demi-cars entered service. Numbered 8 & 9, they lasted until 1921. One regularly worked the Windmill Street service, as shown in this view at the outer terminus by the Old Prince of Orange pub. The Gravesend & Northfleet Electric Tramways closed in February 1929 and was replaced by buses. (Postcard by Thornton Bros, New Brompton, about 1908.)

Tram Terminus, Windmill St, Gravesend

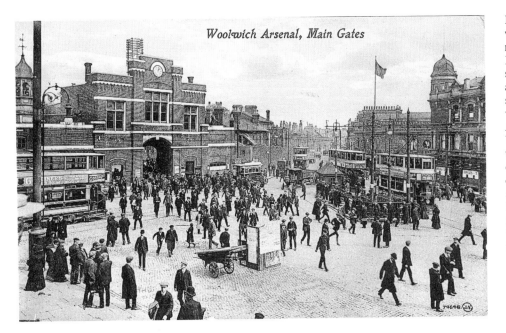

Woolwich Arsenal, Main Gates

London County Council ran an extensive network of trams around Woolwich, and through-running to the adjoining Bexley, Erith and Dartford lines was eventually possible. The system passed to London Transport in 1933, and the last trams ran in 1952. This busy scene shows Beresford Square at lunchtime with workers leaving the main gate of Woolwich Arsenal. The trams are LCC 'E1' Class 70-seat bogie cars, introduced in 1907, of which one thousand were built, and on the far right one of a hundred 62-seat truck-mounted 'M' Class of 1911. Also visible are a steam lorry and a single-deck version of the London General B-type bus. Over 5,000 of these were built, mostly as double-deckers. (Published by Valentine, Dundee, and sent from Woolwich to East Malling, 19th June 1915.)

10

Also at Woolwich is one of two foot-tunnels under the Thames (the other is at Greenwich). The tunnel was authorised under the Thames Tunnel (North & South Woolwich) Act, 1909, and was opened by The London County Council in 1912. A spiral staircase and a lift were provided at each end with identical round brick-built entrances: that on the south side is now hidden by the new Riverside Leisure Centre. This view of the interior provides one of the most boring postcards one can find! (This card was sent, like the previous card, from Woolwich to East Malling, this time on 1st October 1915. The sender was working at the Arsenal, and writing to his mother, with the post office coping with only her name and the village for the address.)

Another tunnel, but at the opposite end of the county, is Shakespeare Cliff Tunnel, the rather impressive entry into Dover of the South Eastern Railway's mainline. Emerging from the tunnel is a down boat train hauled by No. 730, a Wainwright 'D' Class 4-4-0 engine of 1901. (This particular card has no publisher shown, but the same photograph was used on a South Eastern & Chatham Railway official postcard, about 1906.)

This interesting map card shows the development of the transport system in the Dover and Folkestone areas at the turn of the century. Noteworthy are the proposed course of the Channel Tunnel, and the closed Elham Valley and Sandgate branches, while the East Kent Light Railway has yet to be built. The inset shows the Toll Road at Folkestone, which was roughly the line of route by which the SER at one time hoped to reach Folkestone Harbour from Sandgate. (A Walker Geographical Series using a Bartholomew map, which is basically the same format as their maps today, postally used 14th September 1903, Folkestone to Erith.)

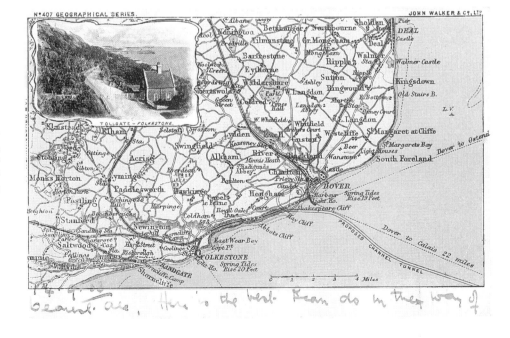

The first of many views of Dover Harbour. This is the Admiralty Pier, started in 1847 and completed in 1871, although both South Eastern and London, Chatham & Dover boat-trains were using it by 1863. This view shows a paddle-steamer nearest the camera, with a newer turbine steamer behind. The vast crowd of people is presumably disembarking from a ferry, although the absence of a boat-train is surprising. At this time there were paddle-steamer berths on the seaward side of the pier, presumably only used in good weather! (Published by Whorwell, Dover, about 1906.)

A general shot of Dover Harbour. On the far left is the Southern (or Island) Breakwater completed in 1909; pointing seawards is the Prince of Wales Pier finished in 1902, while the Admiralty Pier was extended, as the Western Arm, about 1903. The large building distant right was The Lord Warden Hotel, while nearby work has started on reclaiming the site of Dover Marine Station. In the foreground is the Tidal Basin and the Granville Dock. (A HB's F&L postcard No. 438, about 1911.)

General view of Dover Harbour.

A similar postcard taken much later. The Lord Warden Hotel is in the centre, with Dover Marine Station, opened in January 1915, beyond. Another new feature is the elevated road, suitably named Viaduct Road. The girder bridge crossed the railway spur from Folkestone towards Dover Priory Station. On the seashore, with the straddle-crane, is Dover Town Station, while a disused paddle-steamer berth can be seen on the old Admiralty Pier. (Postcard published by E. Williamson, Dover, late 1920s.)

Dover briefly had the status of a trans-Atlantic port. These large boats used the seaward end of the Prince of Wales Pier. The Hamburg Amerika Line made a trial berthing in July 1903, and as a result decided to transfer the Southampton call to Dover in 1904, with four boats in each direction a week. Their largest ship was the *Deutschland*, new in 1900 and able to carry nearly 2,000 passengers. It is shown here on one of its visits to Dover. (A Dover Express photograph; Great Britain and Ireland postcard about 1905.)

S.S. AMERIKA AT DOVER

An even larger ship, for 4,000 passengers, the SS *Amerika* entered service in August 1905. A railway line was provided the length of the Prince of Wales Pier, for the benefit of the boat trains, which often conveyed less than a hundred passengers. The Hamburg Amerika Liners reverted to Southampton in 1907, although smaller Red Funnel Line boats ran from 1904 to 1914. (The publisher of this card is unknown; it was sent from Dover to Harrow on 19th September 1908.)

A view from the sea-front, showing the SS *Prinz Sigismund* at Dover on 27th July 1903. In the distance work extending the Western Arm can be seen, while the Southern Breakwater has yet to be started. The narrow gap subsequently created here was one of the reasons why the liners ceased to use Dover. In the foreground the enclosed horse-buses are different from the brakes favoured elsewhere on the Kent coast. (Published by J. Davis, London.)

Dover.   The Prince of Wales Pier, showing the first American Liner that has called there.

1248

Swedish S.S. Olaus Olsson which ran into the Southern Breakwater on Oct. 20th, 1906.
Lying in the Commercial Harbour, October 21st, after the accident.
"Dover Express" Series, No. 80

With the enclosure of the harbour, just two narrow entrances were left and these have been subject to a number of collisions over the years. Even before this work had been finished, a Swedish freighter loaded with timber hit the construction piers of the Southern Breakwater on 20th October 1906. This postcard shows the SS *Olaus Olsson* in the harbour the day after the accident. The photograph was taken from the Prince of Wales Pier, looking towards the Admiralty Pier. (The Dover Express series, sent from Dover to Ramsgate, 7th November 1906.)

This view shows the damage done to the temporary pier used for the construction of the breakwaters. The seaward side of two main cross-girders was completely demolished. For scale note the men on the platforms on the right of the picture. (No publisher or date, although it can be assumed the photograph was taken in 1906, soon after the accident.)

The Cliffs & Wrecked Preussen

A very famous wreck was that of the *Preussen*. She was built as late as 1902, being a strange mixture of old and new — and a steel-hulled sailing ship. In bad weather in November 1910 she was rammed by a cross-channel ferry off Newhaven, but ironically she drifted out of control onto the cliffs at Dover and eventually broke up. This interesting postcard is made up of two photographs and heavily retouched, as this sort of view could only be obtained by a seagull! If you have 'Kent Transport In Old Postcards' another view of this wreck shows its true position! (HB's F&L 439, posted August 1912, Dover to Earlsfield.)

The busy sealanes round Dover no doubt kept the lifeboat active and the launching of the lifeboat was always a popular subject for photographers. Here a crowd, mainly of children, watch the Dover lifeboat being launched from the beach, about where the Hoverport is today. Observe how basic the boat is and the large crew; the sea is calm — there was no breakwater at this time — so perhaps this was an exercise. (Published by F.G.O. Stuart, and sent from Temple Ewell to Tunbridge Wells on 29th December 1905, 'wishing you a Happy New Year'.)

The Lord Warden Hotel was built facing the Admiralty Pier and had over 150 bedrooms. It was mainly a staging post for Continental travellers, offering a cabin registration service on the boats and registering luggage to Brussels and all Europe. Porters met the Continental Mail Boats and every train arriving at Dover Town Station. On its closure it became Southern House, the British Rail (later Sealink) Offices in Dover. (HB's F&L 406, posted on 25th April 1911 from Dover to Cambridge.)

The Lord Warden Hotel also advertised its sea views. This postcard was taken from the Hotel looking down the pier. In the harbour work is taking place on land reclamation for Dover Marine Station, while another 'D' Class locomotive waits by the signal box on the London, Chatham & Dover Railway's connection to the pier. (HB's F&L 404, sent under cover, i.e. in an envelope, 11th April 1912.)

15

When the Southern Railway was formed in 1923, its first standard locomotive design was the King Arthur Class 4-6-0, which was based largely on London & South Western tradition. Seen at Dover Marine Station is 771 'Sir Sagramore', one of the 1925 batch built by the North British Locomotive Company and fitted with the larger eight-wheeled tender. These engines were later fitted with large smoke deflectors which altered their appearance considerably. (No date or publisher.)

The first station out of Dover on the South Eastern mainline was, after 1908, Folkestone Warren Halt. This rather basic facility could have served only walkers along the coastal footpaths, although it was staffed with a small ticket office. Today the platforms are still used by railway staff on sea-defence work. (No publisher, date about 1910.)

S. E. Turbine Steamer Leaving Folkestone

Folkestone was also an important cross-channel harbour, but failed to develop as fast as Dover. This was because of a slightly longer sea route, and the poorer rail access. The harbour was owned by the South Eastern Railway and of the English boats only their ferries used the port. In this view looking townwards from the end of the pier, a departing steamer makes considerable clag. (No publisher, about 1910.)

In 1899 a joint operating committee was formed by the previously competing SER and LC&DR, which then became known as the South Eastern & Chatham Railway. About 1904 they issued a set of postcards depicting various aspects of their activities, featuring stations, boats and trains. All were printed by McCorquodale & Co. Ltd, who also printed railway timetables. This one shows a luxurious and incredibly ornate interior of a first-class drawing room coach of the London to Folkestone boat-train. (Sent from Langton to Yalding, 1906.)

Less glamorous was this cargo-only paddle-steamer, the SS *Maidstone*, shown leaving Dover Harbour. Most, if not all, of their ships at the time were included in these postcards. (Sent under cover — no date.)

Boat-trains and the new 'D' Class engines also feature strongly in the series. Here a coast-bound boat express is shown at the London end of Orpington, on the mainline route via Tonbridge and Ashford. (Unused.)

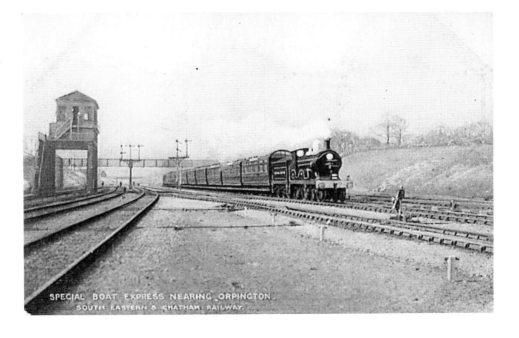

17

The somewhat remote Sandling Junction station, near Hythe, appears twice in this series. This view shows the ubiquitous Wainwright 'D' Class 4-4-0 on a stopping up main-line service, while the Sandgate branch is worked by a 'C' or 'Q1' Class 0-6-0 loco. Here the up branch train has crossed to the down branch platform to give a cross platform connection with mainline. (Unused.)

The second card of Sandling Junction shows a down boat-train seen from the down branch platforms. The signal box controlling the junction can be seen, while the tall double signal on the up main platform allowed drivers to see at least one arm clear of the station footbridge. (Unused.)

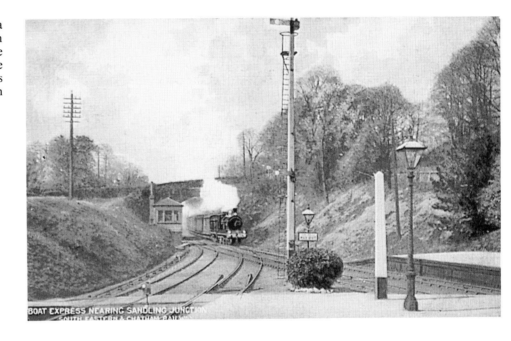

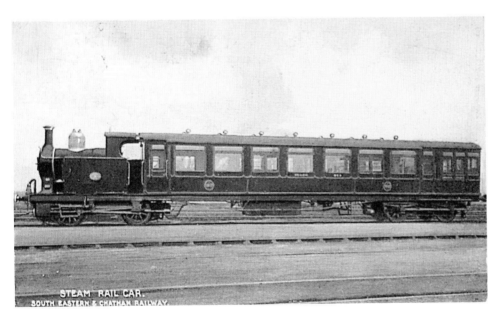

The last card of this series shows one of the unsuccessful steam railcars, introduced in 1905. Eight were built in an attempt to save money on branch lines, working on such routes as Chatham Central, Sandgate and the Elham Valley line. They consisted of a Kitson 0-4-0 engine unit joined to a 56-seat coach. They could be driven from either end, with the fireman staying in the engine cab. However, they suffered from rough riding, being underpowered, and were forever dirty as the coach part had to go to the engine shed each night with the engine! The last survived only until 1920. (Posted from Wateringbury to Brenzett, 15th April 1907.)

A later view of Sandling taken from the road overbridge. High up on the right the roof of the Station Master's house can be seen, while lower down the main station building is on the up branch platform, nearest the approach road. Although the Sandgate branch opened in 1874, no station was built here until 1888. Prior to this main line connections were made at Westenhanger station. In this picture the engine of the branch train is already on the Sandgate end ready to depart. (HB's F&L No. 7, sent Folkestone to London, 7th November 1918.)

Ashford became an important centre of the SER, with the main works and four lines, to London, Hastings, Dover and Ramsgate to serve it, as well as the LC&DR line from Maidstone. The level of traffic resulted in the provision of four platforms and two through lines. This picture is taken looking towards Dover, showing the down main platform and the two through lines. The fine array of semaphore signals at the country end controlled the junctions. Today the layout remains basically unaltered, but the station buildings were totally rebuilt in the 1960s, as part of the Kent Coast Electrification Scheme. (W.H. Smith's postcard, sent from Ashford to Bromley Green on 8th July 1915.)

The original South Eastern Railway's mainline ran almost dead straight from Ashford to just outside Redhill. One of the smaller stations on this section is at Staplehurst. This Edwardian view is taken from the road overbridge looking towards London. The staggered platform arrangement was common SER practice at these smaller stations (examples like Rye and East Farleigh still exist). The station was considerably rebuilt for Kent Coast Electrification. The platforms were extended for longer trains, thus ending the stagger. The goods yard on the left became the station car park, but some of the goods sheds survived, as did a fine South Eastern & Chatham Railway iron gate, which must have replaced the wooden gates and fences not long after this photograph was taken. (Published by J.T. Powell, Staplehurst, and posted 30th August 1909 from Staplehurst to Deal.)

19

When the SER reached Paddock Wood in 1842, there was only farmland and the station was originally called Maidstone Road. The first station building was this single-storey block on the up side. This view is taken from the approach road in the days when more horses than cars would use it; now the goods yard on the left is a car park. In 1988 the station was extensively modernised and a new entrance hall provided. (Published by G.A. Cooper, Maidstone, and sent from Paddock Wood to Sydenham on 6th September 1917.)

Paddock Wood grew to be a major junction with lines to Maidstone and Hawkhurst. This elevated view is from the junction signal box, looking towards the station and London. On the left is the Hawkhurst Branch platform, while the Maidstone trains use the other bay platform, with the main goods yard, still used today, on the far right. Observe the rake of ancient coaches in the yard and the shunting loco standing in the down platform. (W.H. Smith's Kingsway Real Photo Series and sent from Five Oak Green to Great Chart, 9th February 1915.)

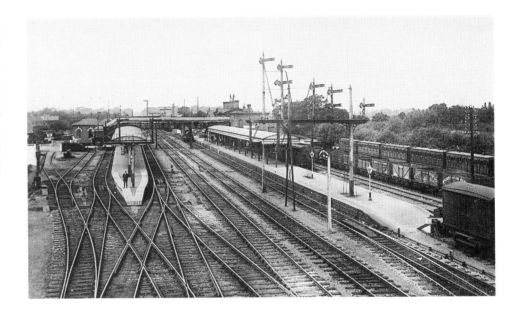

A view of Paddock Wood from the opposite end, taken from the road bridge and showing the former West Yard signal box. An up train is running non-stop on the through line, while the junction signal box and its signals can be seen at the other end of the station. On the down platform the later and larger buildings were demolished with electrification and replaced with a smaller modern building. At this stage the platforms were extended to take ten coach trains, and have recently been further lengthened to take twelve coach trains. The platforms now occupy all the available space between the road bridge and the junction to Maidstone. (No publisher or date.)

Paddock Wood was the centre of the hop traffic, both in terms of special passenger trains for the hop-pickers and the dispatch of the hops for market. This busy scene in the East Yard at Paddock Wood shows no less than three horse-drawn carts delivering hop pockets for transhipment. Those already loaded on the first wagon have come from a farm at nearby Brenchley. Although they still have to be tied down and sheeted they seem to be loaded very high and close to the loading gauge. (Published by J. Valentines, Dundee, about 1905.)

A final postcard of the railway at Paddock Wood shows an accident at the London end of the station on 5th May 1919. It is not clear what has happened, but loco No. 61 is derailed on the down line under the bridge, with a goods brake behind it. The remains of some parcel vans can also be seen by the bridge, so one possibility is a freight train colliding with some parcel vans that had been left or run on the main line. A good crowd has gathered on the road bridge to watch the clearing up. (Published by Allwork, Tonbridge.)

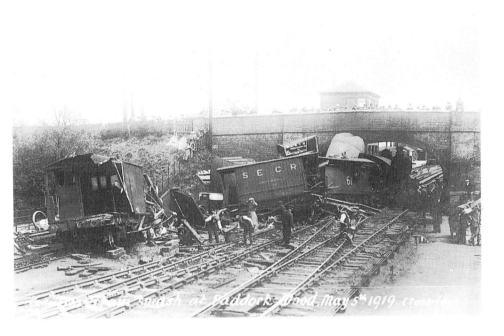

A rare 'in memoriam' postcard for a more serious accident at Tonbridge on 5th March 1909, resulting in the death of a Loco Inspector and a Fireman. The accident happened at the London end of Tonbridge Station, when the 9.00 boat-train from Charing Cross to Dover, running via Orpington, hit the 8.30 from Charing Cross via Redhill, which had passed a signal at danger. Prompt action by two station staff at Tonbridge prevented an up express from Margate running into the wreckage. The Royal Train conveying the King to Dover had to be stopped at Orpington and diverted via Chatham. (Published by W. Gothard, Barnsley.)

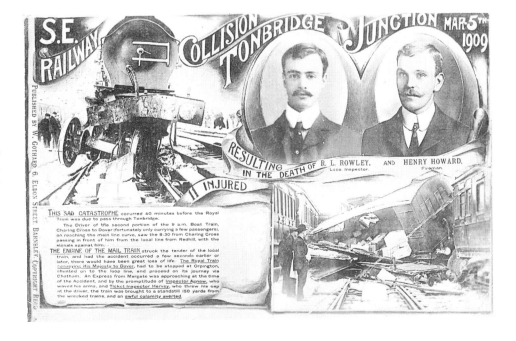

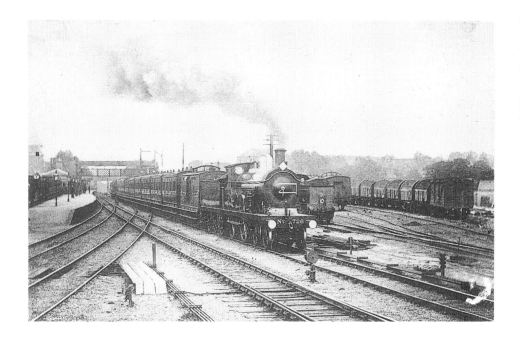

This postcard features another Wainwright 'D' Class on a down boat-train. This is No. 726, built by Sharp & Stewart in 1901. The location is Grove Park and the picture was taken just before the main line was quadrupled in about 1905. The line joining on the left of the picture is the Bromley North branch. (No publisher, c1904.)

This view is taken a little further down the line at Chislehurst, and a few years later, with the four tracks in use. This time the train is the down Hastings American Car (i.e. Pullman) Express. The loco is again a Wainwright 'D' Class, this example being built in Glasgow by Dübs & Co. in 1903. The postcard is a coloured type which shows the full glory of South Eastern & Chatham loco livery; red buffers and sole bars, matt black smokebox, brass dome; main areas of paintwork were dark green lined out in gold. (Published by the Locomotive Publishing Co. Ltd, London, about 1910.)

The magnificence of Southern steam! Heading the 2 p.m. Victoria to Dover boat through Orpington is No. 865 'Sir John Hawkins', a Lord Nelson Class 4-6-0 engine built at East-leigh in 1929. Orpington is the end of the four track section from London, and was for many years the end of the electrified suburban system. An electric unit has just left for London and is passing the signal box; note the lower quadrant signal at the end of the platform, still cleared for its passage. (Published by the Locomotive Publishing Co. Ltd, London, about 1935.)

The Medway Valley Line from Paddock Wood to Strood has some gems of stations. The line was opened from Paddock Wood to Maidstone in 1844, but only temporary-type buildings were provided initially. When the line was extended to Strood in 1856, fine stone or brick stations were provided throughout the line. Unfortunately that at Yalding was burnt out in 1893, and replaced by this more modest building, which was similar to other country stations built around this time. The signal box was removed in 1986 and the crossing converted to open light control, to much protesting by locals. Otherwise the station had many of the features found at other stations on the line, like the goods shed and staggered platforms. There was also an end loading dock on the far left of the picture. (Published by Lawrence, Tonbridge, and postally used 28th July 1905, Tonbridge to Battersea.)

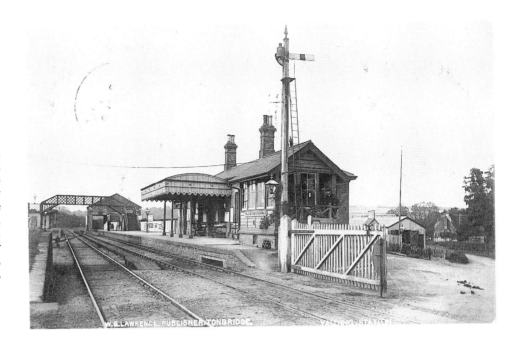

The king of all the stations on the line is Wateringbury. The main station building, on the down side, used red brick with ashlared Caen stone quoins, and lofty hexagonal chimney stacks in Victorian Gothic style. (Aylesford is in a similar style, but with ragstone instead of bricks.) Beyond the station building is the Station Master's house, which is an older building — possibly pre-railway — although matching chimneys have been provided. The general aspect of the station has changed little from this view taken from the approach road, but the grassy area in the foreground is now the station car park. (No publisher, sent Wateringbury to Yalding, 14th October 1909.)

A trackside view of the station is equally impressive. The splendid gas-lamp and the aged four-wheeled passenger coach in the goods yard have gone, but the staggered platforms remain. Alas the shelter on the up platform was replaced in 1989 by a Network South East red greenhouse shelter. A footbridge now joins the platforms. (Published by G.A. Cooper, Maidstone, and sent 3rd August 1915 from Wateringbury to Braintree.)

23

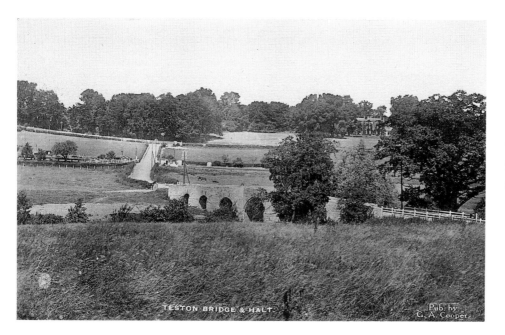

Two halts were opened on the line in 1909. The one at Beltring survives today, but Teston Crossing Halt closed in 1959. Short wooden platforms were provided by the crossing keeper's house. The crossing keeper would have issued the tickets. Teston Village is up the hill on the far left of the postcard, and the bus service would have been a more attractive prospect for the villagers. The large house on the right is Barham Court, while in the foreground the fine medieval ragstone bridge over the River Medway can be seen. (Publisher is G.A. Cooper, Maidstone, c1910.)

The first station at Maidstone (West) lasted only from 1844 to 1856, when it was realigned for the extension to Strood, although some of the original buildings were only demolished in 1986. The new layout was restricted by the short tunnel under the Tonbridge and London Roads, at the Strood end of the station. Only one through line was provided instead of the two that were standard at major SER stations, and bay platforms were only at the Paddock Wood end of the station, despite the Strood section of the line becoming the busiest. Today one bay platform has been removed, and the other is used only for parcel vans. Also the platform awning is much shortened, the footbridge has been relocated and coloured-light signals have replaced the semaphores. (No publisher, about 1906.)

On the Strood section of the line, Cuxton is of a similar style to Wateringbury, but much smaller. The staff house, with its attractive bay window, is an integral part of the station building. The wooden signal box dates from about 1890, when block signals were installed on the line, and is shortly due for replacement, when control of the whole line will be transferred to Maidstone West signal box. Today the structure of the station is little altered, the footbridge between the platforms and a new shelter on the down platform being the most obvious changes. (Published by F.E. Chalklen, Post Office, Cuxton, and posted from Cuxton to Clapham, 3rd August 1910.)

Westerham provided an ideal example of a country branch line terminal station. Three elderly four-wheeled coaches wait in the sole platform to form the branch service, while the loco is being prepared in the one-engine shed in the distance. A small goods shed and single-storey wooden station building were provided. The line opened in 1881 from a junction with the main line at Dunton Green, and was just under five miles long, with two intermediate stations. It closed in 1961, and today much of its route has been obliterated by the M25 motorway. (Published by Fuller of ?, sent from Gillingham to Braintree, 5th July 1914.)

Grove Ferry station was a substantial affair on the SER line of 1846 between Canterbury and Ramsgate. It was connected by the ferry to the Grove Ferry Hotel, but otherwise it served only a few isolated farmsteads; it was however a popular spot for trippers from Canterbury and Thanet. Note the large and neatly laid out garden of the crossing keeper's cottage. Today the station (closed in 1966) has gone and the ferry has been replaced by a bridge, but the hotel remains. (Published by J.G. Charlton, Canterbury, and posted Wickham to Dover, 7th September 1906.)

Another, somewhat curious, postcard of Grove Ferry. It was taken from the hotel side of the river and shows the ferry in action; it was a simple raft, hand-operated along a permanently fitted hawser. Across the bank is the station, the main building to the right and the crossing keeper's cottage on the left. The reference on the postcard to the Marist Brothers' College is beyond my research, but was not the station building! There are other cards in this series which show the Brothers at work. Equally puzzling is the publisher of the postcard; it has all the hallmarks of the work of a French photographer and publisher of Russian descent, L. Levitsky (later known as Levy), but lacks his usual trademark of L.L. after the caption; indeed his work in England is otherwise limited to major tourist locations like Canterbury and Dover. The card dates from about 1904.

CRANBROOK STATION, KENT.

The Cranbrook & Paddock Wood Railway was incorporated in 1877, but the company failed to attract enough capital. The line was finally constructed by the SER, opening from Paddock Wood to Goudhurst in October 1892, and to Hawkhurst in September 1893. The line was generally single track and was noted for its sharp curves and steep gradients, as it climbed into the High Weald. The line was busy with freight traffic, especially with hops in September. Passenger demand was never great, mainly due to the remote locations of the stations; only Horsmonden was close to the village it served. Cranbrook was in fact nearly two miles from the town at the hamlet of Hartley, and even then had its own approach road of some length. A passing loop was provided, but there was only one platform, preventing two passenger trains crossing here. The signal box and station building are like the rebuilt Yalding Station of the same era, but the three-storey Station Master's house is an unusual feature. The line closed on 11th June 1961, the final day of steam in Kent. Much of interest remains of this line, particularly here and at Hawkhurst, but most is private property. (Postcard by Photochrom Co. Ltd, Tunbridge Wells, unused; dates from about 1906.)

The bleak area of the Romney Marsh was served by a branch line from Appledore, on the Ashford to Hastings line. Lydd was opened in December 1880. The line closed for passengers on 6th March 1967, but has been retained for aggregate traffic and the nuclear flasks from Dungeness Power Station. As a result the platforms and station building remain, albeit rather overgrown and derelict. (Published by G.A. Cooper, Maidstone, about 1912.)

Lydd Station.

Shepherdswell Station.

The SER's monopoly of Kent lasted just under twenty years. The London, Chatham & Dover Railway started as the East Kent Railway, opening a line from the SER at Strood to Canterbury in 1858. However, by route extensions and running powers over other companies' lines in London, a Victoria to Dover service was introduced from 22nd July 1861. Shepherdswell, just outside Dover, was opened the same day. It later became the junction station for the East Kent Light Railway, whose trains ran from the far right in this view looking towards Canterbury. (Postcard by W. Coppen, about 1912.)

26

End of the line across Romney Marsh was Dungeness, again opened in 1880, although passenger trains did not run until 1882. In 1884 a branch was opened to New Romney from a junction over a mile from Lydd. This double-ended branch made it difficult to operate and the situation was rationalised from 1937, when the New Romney branch was rerouted nearer the coast serving Lydd-on-Sea, and Dungeness was closed to passengers. The postcard shows one of twelve Stirling 'A' Class 4-4-0 locos built at Ashford between 1879 and 1881 and regularly used on this route. They were withdrawn by 1909. (Published by A.E. Shaw — no location known — and posted from Dover to Chatham, 23rd July 1907.)

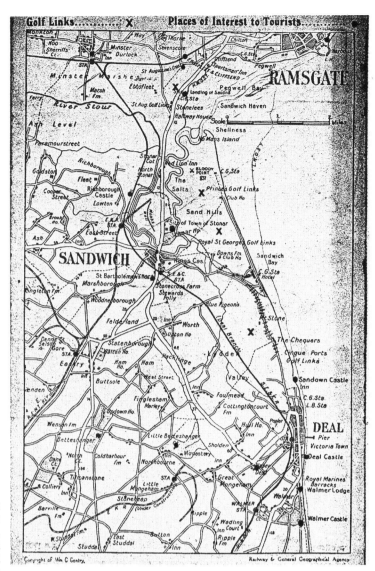

This map card of the Sandwich area is particularly interesting as it shows part of the EKLR. This line was built largely to carry coal from the Kent Coalfield, although it also conveyed agricultural products, and from 1916 to 1948 offered a passenger service. The first line opened from Shepherdswell to Eastry and Wingham Colliery in 1912. Eastry to Sandwich Road followed in 1916 and this was extended across the River Stour to Richborough in 1929. In 1925 the line to Wingham was extended to Canterbury Road. Planned extensions to Canterbury and the line shown as 'under construction' on the map to Mongeham were never built. The last section of EKLR, between Shepherdswell and Tilmanstone Colliery, closed in March 1984. (Postcard by Wm. C. Gentry, Railway & General Agency, 24 Surrey Road, Margate, dated about 1930.)

Gillingham Station (originally New Brompton, and renamed New Brompton & Gillingham in 1886) was slightly east of the present location and featured only two platforms. The station was rebuilt and a third platform provided as part of the 1939 electrification scheme, when the station took its current name. This view is looking from the London end of the up platform; the main station building was located on the down platform, with the entrance from Station Road. (Published by Thornton Bros, New Brompton, and posted 30th August 1906, Gillingham to Borough Green.)

Chatham Station is in a very cramped location between Chatham Tunnel and Fort Pitt Tunnel, and is also spanned by two road bridges. It was built with four running lines and five platform faces and a signal box at each end. A number of ancillary buildings were provided at track level, including a smithy, with the ticket office located on the over-bridge. The postcard shows the view from the London end of the station. When the platforms were lengthened to take twelve coach electric sets, the platforms ran almost from portal to portal. The up platform loop (nearest camera) and sidings were removed and became a car park. The down platform loop became a siding, connected at the country end and used by parcel trains; this too has now been removed. (W.N. Eastgate Series, Rochester, postally used 7th May 1908, Herne Bay to Dover.)

To obtain a direct route to London the LCDR main line leaves the Medway Valley with a five mile climb at 1 in 100, initially traversing a rural landscape. Some stations were provided like Fawkham, here seen from across the ripening corn. It opened in June 1872, some eleven years after the line, following a donation from a local landowner. At that stage only one house was visible from the station, the next building to appear was the Railway Tavern! The station was several miles from Fawkham, and in the parish of Longfield with a population of less than 200. It was rebuilt after a fire in 1900. During this century many houses have been built in this area, giving a regular commuter traffic. In 1961 it was renamed Longfield for Fawkham & Hartley and in 1968 just Longfield. (W.H. Smith's Kingsway Real Photo Series, about 1910.)

When the LC&DR opened a line to Sevenoaks in 1862, a new station was provided at the junction with the main line. This was known initially as Sevenoaks Junction. It was located over a mile from the small village of Swanley, but as the settlement grew into a suburban town, much of the development was attracted towards the station. The station was renamed Swanley Junction in 1871. This postcard shows the station about 1910 looking down the main line on the left and towards Sevenoaks and Maidstone on the right. The station was totally rebuilt in its present location, on the London side of the junction, for the 1939 electrification scheme to Gillingham and Maidstone East. The old station would have been unable to cope with the electric service, which required Gillingham and Maidstone trains to split and join here. Today some rubble in the 'V' of the junction is the only sign of the old station. (Another W.H. Smith postcard, sent Swanley to Hastings in 1913.)

Malling Station, Kent.

The LC&DR line to Maidstone East opened in 1874, with stations at Kemsing, Wrotham, Malling and Barming. This postcard shows Malling (now West Malling), again about 1910. The low building nearest the camera was part of the original building. It was symmetrical when built, but about 1890 the station was enlarged and the second gable end of the single-storied structure was removed, and a larger two-storeyed ticket office and station house were built. Wrotham — now Borough Green — was similarly rebuilt, but is a mirror image, being on the down platform, rather than the up as at West Malling. Barming has not been extended and retains its original building in the same style. West Malling station has changed little since this view; in 1986 the station was restored and the wooden-fronted part of the first station was removed to make an open shelter. The West Malling by-pass opened in 1988, and crosses over the line just beyond the station. (Postcard by Stedman of West Malling, sent 10th August 1912, East Malling to Dalton-in-Furness.)

At Maidstone the LC&DR crossed the River Medway by a girder bridge, known as the High Level Bridge. The station itself was built on land previously the site of the worst slums in the town. This postcard shows how frail the original structure was; it was replaced in 1927, to allow larger locomotives to use the route, particularly on boat-trains diverted from the Tonbridge route. The small tank loco on the bridge was no doubt the station pilot, which would have been busy serving the goods yards at the station — now car parks — and possibly banking trains on the stiff climb to Barming. (A Young & Cooper, Maidstone, postcard, postally used 5th August 1913, Maidstone to Hildenborough.)

HIGH LEVEL BRIDGE, MAIDSTONE.

The third major railway company to serve the area covered by this book was the London, Brighton & South Coast. Its main interest lay in the routes to the Sussex coast, and it generally had a good relationship with the SER, having shared running lines and stations from the early days. Competition did break out with respect to Tunbridge Wells, where the LB&SCR offered an alternative route to London via Edenbridge and Croydon. They also provided cross country routes to Three Bridges and Brighton via Uckfield. Their station was a splendid brick building, complete with clock tower, which opened in 1866. It was remote from the town, beyond the Pantiles, and later became Tunbridge Wells West. As Beeching cuts took hold in Sussex the service was reduced to a Tonbridge – Eridge shuttle with connections for Uckfield and London. Because of the substandard sized, single-track tunnel under Tunbridge Wells the line was not suitable for electrification, and it finally closed on 6th July 1985. The station, gas-lit to the end, stands with its windows boarded up, in forlorn grandeur. (Valentines of Dundee postcard, about 1905.)

When the LB&SCR introduced motor trains on various routes, it attempted to increase revenue by opening new halts. These could be built cheaply as they were unstaffed and only one coach long. Their line from Tunbridge Wells passed close to the High Rocks, an outcrop of sandstone popular with climbers and one such halt was provided here. Originating traffic must have been small, but it was popular with visitors in the summer. It opened in 1907 and closed in 1952. (Published by Rabson Bros, Tunbridge Wells, sent Tunbridge Wells to Canada, 27th November 1907.)

Another LB&SCR station to be just inside Kent is Ashurst, opened in 1888. It was once on the main line to Eastbourne and Tunbridge Wells, but today is served by the hourly Uckfield to Oxted diesel trains, the sole remaining line of the once extensive network in this area. It is a typical country station of the LB&SCR, with many similarities of style of construction found in their major stations, on a grander scale. (No publisher, except J.R.! and sent to Yalding on 28th June 1912.)

The Kent and East Sussex Railway opened from Robertsbridge in 1900. The line reached Tenterden Town in 1903 and Headcorn in 1905, but further expansion plans did not materialize. The line was one of several light railways to be managed by Col. Holman Stephens. Its existence was always precarious, using secondhand stock, and it became bankrupt in 1931. The line finally closed in 1961, but in 1974 the first section reopened in preservation. Rolvenden Station was the operating centre of the K&ESR, housing the engine shed, but Tenterden Town was the principal station. This postcard shows 2-4-0 tank engine 'Northiam' outside Rolvenden shed, with the simple single-platform station behind. (Published by The Locomotive Publishing Co. Ltd, London, about 1920.)

The Romney, Hythe & Dymchurch Railway was the product of two rich railway enthusiasts, Capt. John Howey and Count Louis Zborowski. It was opened in stages between 1926 and 1928, and operated as a miniature version of a mainline railway, using 15-inch gauge one third scale locomotives. It originally provided an all year service, but now operates during the summer only, except for a special service for pupils at New Romney School. Exchange of stock with the Ravenglass & Eskdale Railway, the only other line of this gauge, is common and recently stock has been supplied to the Garden Festivals, held alternate years to rejuvenate run down areas. The postcard shows No. 8 'Hurricane', a 4-6-2 of 1927, on a Hythe Chamber of Commerce special, on the terminal loop at Dungeness. (Postcard by RH&DR itself, about 1935.)

Kent also had many industrial railways associated with docks, quarries or factories. The Holborough Cement Works at Snodland had its own line linking the works complex with the chalk quarry at Upper Halling, about two miles away. The track of this line can just be seen in the bottom left of this postcard, while the crossing keeper poses outside his rotunda-style box. (Published by A.N. Hambrook, Snodland, about 1912.)

Holborough Road, Snodland.

A. N. Hambrook's Photo Series

Captain Charles Place, DSO, sits at the steering wheel of his 1907 Humber 15 h.p. car. When this car was registered his address was given as the RE Brompton Barracks, Chatham, and the body was described as green 'Roi des Belges', apparently after the King of Belgium had specified this type of bodywork. Note that the spare wheel, which should be on the hoop next to the driver, and all the lights, are missing. The car was only six months old when this postcard was sent; it was taken at an army encampment possibly in North Wales. (Posted 26th September 1907, Trawsfynydd to Gravesend; no publisher.)

As the rail network spread across the country from the 1840s onwards the mail coaches soon ceased, with most mail being carried by train. The Post Office however began to experiment with road transport in the Edwardian era. This Milnes-Daimler lorry commenced a London to Ramsgate Mail Service on 15th July 1908. This postcard was taken at Madeira Drive, Ramsgate, on the first day. The lorry was supplied and operated on behalf of the Post Office by Tillings, the London bus operator. (Unused and no publisher.)

As well as its agricultural use, steam power was used for heavy haulage and construction work. This postcard shows a Rochester built Aveling & Porter steam-roller at work on road improvements. It was owned by the Kent County Council (No. 8), as shown by the brass plate on the side, although the white horse ('Invicta') on the front was the logo of Aveling & Porter. (No date or publisher, but about 1906.)

Walter Bannister had a garage business in King Street, Maidstone, and from about 1904 to 1910 he built a number of these single seat three-wheelers under the name of 'Unecar'. This postcard shows his daughter in one of his products outside his garage. Interestingly, this postcard was sent in 1932 to the editor of 'The Motor', with the sender commenting on Bannister's role in the evolution of the light car. (Posted 20th March 1932, Sutton to London, no publisher.)

Miss V. Bannister, Maidstone, on her "Unecar"

Another strange vehicle was this mobile church, although in its running condition it would have looked much like a normal van. It was built by Gibson & Brown of Tunbridge Wells, who had this postcard produced for publicity about 1925.

This fine machine, registered D1034 on 18th March 1904, was a 7 h.p. MMC with a tonneau body and painted dark blue. It was owned by William E. Allen, who lived at 10 Silverhill Road, Ashford. He was the town's Inspector of Weights and Measures, but as the vehicle was licensed as a 'public conveyance', he no doubt had other interests. The MMC (made in Coventry) was one of the more reliable of the early vehicles and this one was registered until 17th October 1916, some twelve and a half years! This vehicle would have sat eleven passengers plus a driver; note the steps for the passengers in the back seat. (No publisher, date or location — Cliftonville?)

During the Great War Crossley produced large numbers of their heavy car chassis for military use. Some were used as staff cars, but many were bodied as field ambulances and after the war many were to be found in civilian use. This postcard shows a Crossley ambulance based at Cranbrook, standing at the Northern end of Cranbrook High Street. (Published by Stickells & Son, Cranbrook, about 1925.)

33

One of my favourite postcards is this view of T. Wood & Son's butchers shop in Sun Street, Canterbury. My justification for including it in this book is the butcher's boy's delivery bike. These were ubiquitous at this time, with almost every butcher, baker and general store having such a delivery service. Some can still be seen today, often using elderly bicycles. Observe the meat and sausages hanging outside the shop! (Publisher unknown; sent 26th June 1916, Canterbury to Ramsgate.)

An equally interesting postcard is this view of the street cleaner in action in Cranbrook High Street with his wooden hand-cart for the rubbish. Two delivery bikes can be seen behind, and the delivery van belonging to H. Jones of Tunbridge Wells, fish, game (& poultry?), was probably associated with the shop offering 'prime roasting chicken from 3/6'. The shops are all decorated with flags and bunting, suggesting a fair or a royal event. (Published by Stickells & Son, Cranbrook, about 1930.)

The Bell Inn at Golden Green, near Tonbridge, has changed little, but the car parked outside would attract some attention today. KL7651 was a Citroen that was supplied by Rootes Ltd of Maidstone to a Miss Corke of Bower Cottage, Sole Street, in 1935. (No publisher, posted 1935, Tonbridge to Battersea.)

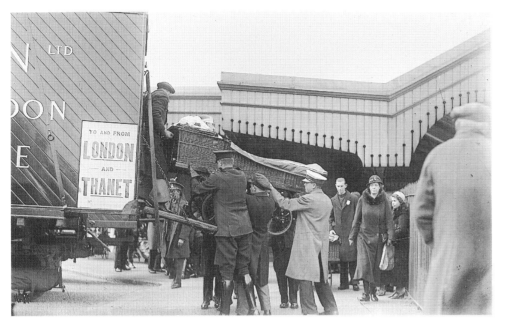

Not the most cheerful postcard to send anyone. This photograph shows a wounded soldier being transferred from a train to a makeshift ambulance at Margate Station sometime in World War I. Thanet had a number of hospitals because of its healthy location and these were supplemented by various hotels for convalescence. The lorry seems to have been used on a carrier service from London to Thanet. (No publisher.)

William Allen was a London based entrepreneur, who operated buses in Essex, Lincolnshire and Worcestershire as well as several locations in Kent. His operations often traded under the 'Silver Queen' name and this postcard shows one of three Thornycroft Charabuses that were operated beween Margate and Ramsgate by the Isle of Thanet Motor Co. Ltd from about 1920. This fleet was sold to East Kent in 1925. (Not used; no publisher.)

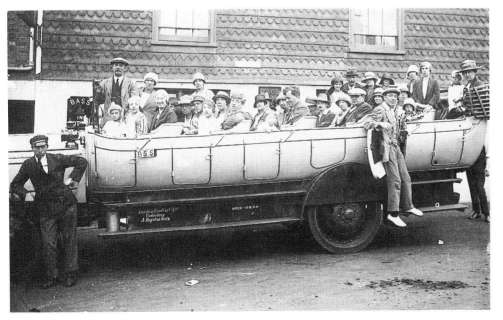

Many charabanc trips ran from Margate and Ramsgate to the attractive village of Minster. Judging by the number of postcards taken of such trips outside the Bell Inn or the church, a photographer must have been stationed here during the summer for this trade. This postcard shows a charabanc at the Bell Inn; the legal lettering on the side is for East Kent, but the light livery suggests a 'Silver Queen' vehicle that has just been taken over. (No date or publisher.)

The Isle of Thanet trams never reached Birchington, so many early bus operators ran between here and Margate. There were many postcards of Birchington Square, and these often showed buses waiting to work the service to Margate. This postcard shows LH8894, a London General 'B' type of 1914. These buses had been sent to France for troop transport during the war and some were sold to other operators on their return. (T. Pointer's Series, postally used 19th April 1916.)

The second view of Birchington shows another 'B' type, LC3772. It is in the same livery as the previous vehicle, but lacks the painted route details. It is not known which firm ran these vehicles, but when the tramway company took over the West Margate Coach Company in 1921, two other buses of this model were in that company's fleet at that stage, so possibly they also operated these two buses. (No publisher, sent from Birchington to Osterley Park, 23rd July 1919.)

This postcard is looking across the Square from the other side. This time a single-deck bus is standing in the usual position prior to operating to Margate. Although the number plate (KT163) can be seen over the near-side rear window, this vehicle has not yet been traced in any records. The registration was issued about 1914. (Postcard published by H. Camburn, Tunbridge Wells, for F. Pointer, Birchington.)

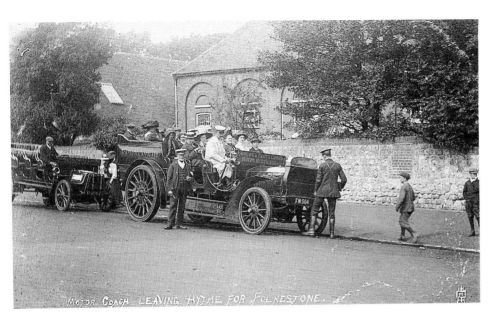

Motor Coach leaving Hythe for Folkestone.

The Folkestone and Hythe area also attracted many early bus operators. By the time of the introduction of registration numbers in 1904, six operators were running seventeen vehicles. Unlike Thanet, where competition was the order, there was a measure of co-operation between operators. A common livery of dark blue (or black) and yellow was adopted. It is thought a co-ordinated timetable was operated — it was certainly proposed. This postcard shows FN504, a 1906 Thames of John Cann's London & South Coast Motor Service Ltd and D2507, a 1906 MMC 20 h.p. of Ernest Wills' Pullman Coaches, at the Hythe terminus. Both these operators started in 1901. The conductor of FN504 prepares to start the engine, while the vehicle behind starts to load; could the gentleman in front holding his watch-chain be an early bus inspector? (Published by Harmer, Sandgate, about 1908.)

When Cann set up the London based L&SCMS in 1906, it was intended to run a number of long distance services to South Coast resorts, using a fleet of powerful 50 h.p. Thames charabancs. In the event they were used on local services at Folkestone or on excursions. Tunbridge Wells was a popular destination and this postcard shows a Thames outside The Castle Hotel, Tunbridge Wells. (Postcard published by The Castle Hotel about 1908.)

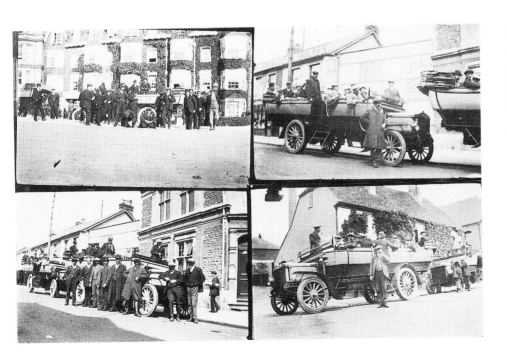

Senior operator in the Folkestone area was T.H. Maltby's Folkestone Motors Ltd, who were running by July 1901. Maltby was also an engineer, with a garage at Sandgate where between about 1908 and 1919 he built his own charabancs. This postcard shows two of Folkestone Motors' Maltby charabancs, D8259 (new July 1912) and D9613 (new April 1913). They were based at the Saracen's Head in Ashford and the postcard records a trip to Tunbridge Wells — the top left photograph is in front of The Castle Hotel again. (No publisher; sent from Ashford to Hamstreet, 15th October 1913.)

37

Maltby also built vehicles for other local operators. This one operated for the Pullman Coaches fleet of Wills of Cheriton and was very similar to those above; it could have been either D7838 of 1912 or D9745 of 1913. The picture was taken in the Wealden village of Brenchley. Wills took over Folkestone Motors about 1924 and sold out to East Kent in 1927. (No publisher or date.)

In 1914 Thomas Tilling was looking for areas outside London to expand; in conjunction with Youngs & Old, Folkestone taxi operators, they set up the Folkestone District Road Car Company, and operated a fleet of about twenty-six Tilling-Stevens buses. This view shows LH8884 running along Sandgate Front when new. Note the horse-tram tracks. This operator was one of five to merge in 1916 to form the East Kent Road Car Company. (Postcard published by F. Frith & Co. Ltd, Reigate, and posted Sandgate to London, 31st August 1925.)

Another constituent company of East Kent was the Deal & District Motor Services. This firm was a British Electric Traction subsidiary and began in April 1908 using Brush buses transferred from Birmingham. This view of Walmer Castle shows one of the single-deck buses suitably posed. The bus company must have had a hand in producing this card, as it has printed above the message section 'Walmer Castle; reached by the Deal—Kingsdown Motor Service. Cars run from Pier Parade frequently. (Posted Deal to Tooting about 1910.)

On 12th July 1906 the worst motoring accident up to that date took place on Handcross Hill, on the London to Brighton road. Ten passengers were killed and the development of long distance bus operation was set back for over ten years. The London Motor Omnibus Company Ltd, trading as 'Vanguard', had been operating a regular service during 1906 between London and Brighton, using Milnes-Daimler double-deckers from their London bus fleet. However, the fateful journey was a special for the annual outing for the St Mary Cray and Orpington Volunteer Firemen. At the top of the hill the brakes failed, the gearbox disintegrated and the driver lost control and ran the bus into the verge. An overhanging branch of a tree was hit by the bus, and the flimsy wooden body of the bus broke up; the upper deck was totally destroyed. The first postcard shows the remains of the bus after the accident, with a traction engine that was used to pull the wreck from the bank. Many of the funerals were held on the 16th and 17th July, the most impressive being that of Mr Hutchings. As well as being a senior member of the fire brigade, he was also the local undertaker. His funeral was watched by almost the entire local population — the shops were shut — and the procession included representatives from other fire brigades and the police. It was so long that it arrived at the church over an hour late. (The postcard publishers had a field day with both these events, but these two cards offer no clue to their publisher.)

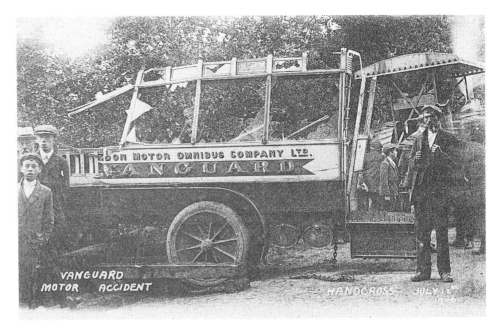

VANGUARD MOTOR ACCIDENT

16433 LONDON RD & WESLEYAN CH.   SOUTHBOROUGH.

The Tunbridge Wells, Southborough & District Omnibus Co. Ltd commenced operations in April 1905 with D1842, a green and yellow Milnes Daimler. The next month a second example, D1959, entered service. However, they were found to be too big and heavy for the old bridge at Tunbridge Wells Central Station and operations ceased by early August 1905, when both vehicles were sold to the Brighton, Hove & Preston United Omnibus Co. Ltd. D1959 remained in service until May 1919. In 1976 the chassis of this vehicle was fitted with a replica body and the vehicle is now preserved in the USA. The postcard shows the bus at what was presumably the Southborough terminus; note the ghostly figure on the right where the plate was under-inked. (Published by Great Britain & Ireland, not used but must be 1905.)

39

Another early bus operator at Tunbridge Wells was Autocar Services Ltd. It commenced operation in 1909, with three double-deckers. During 1910 and 1911 twelve single-deck Leyland buses arrived and after the Great War many more of this type were purchased, two of which are shown in this postcard. They featured full length roof luggage racks, and removable side-windows. Autocar became the major operator in the town, becoming part of the London General empire for a while. It was outside the scope of London Transport on its formation in 1933, and Autocar became part of Maidstone & District. The present M&D garage and Opera House office were both inherited from Autocar. (No publisher or date.)

The Maidstone & District Motor Services Ltd was formed in 1911, and by the start of the Great War they had expanded their services to include this route from Faversham to Ashford. In Faversham buses originally terminated in the cramped Market Place. The bus shown in this postcard is KN7117, a Leyland 'N' built in 1920. Observe the large light on the roof which showed green at night and allowed passengers to recognise their bus. (Published by W.H. Everden, Faversham, about 1922.)

This somewhat faded postcard shows a large outing about to set off from outside the White Horse, Bearsted Green. The front two vehicles are KE3553 and KE4728, Leyland 'N' chara-bancs new to M&D in 1921. Behind are two buses, the leading one of which is a Maidstone-built Tilling-Stevens of 1919 or 1920. (No publisher or date.)

Deal & District (later East Kent) initially terminated in the middle of the road on the Promenade; this postcard shows two East Kent buses awaiting custom; that nearest the camera is on the Dover service; both vehicles are Daimlers dating from about 1920, and were typical of the vehicles used by East Kent to expand operations and replace older buses after the Great War. (Published by J. Welch, Portsmouth, about 1925.)

A view of Dover Market Square when it was the terminus of East Kent's services. Rather frustratingly every bus has its registration number obscured, but from left to right they are: a Tilling-Stevens of about 1925 leaving for Canterbury, a charabanc on the Folkestone route, a Daimler or Tilling-Stevens of about 1920, and a Morris 1-ton 14-seater on a rural run. These were built between 1925 and 1927 and most had bodies constructed by East Kent themselves. (Published by Boots, Pelham Series, after 1925.)

Faversham was a boundary point between East Kent and M&D and buses of both companies can be seen in this view of Court Street. Buses terminate at this location today, although at least two other sites have been used in between. East Kent's offerings on the left are a pair of Tilling-Stevens, with FN9944 of 1929 leading. M&D's long service to Dartford (which was cut back to Gravesend in 1933, on the formation of London Transport) was worked by KR1721, a Leyland Titan TD1 of 1930. (No publisher or date).

This Maidstone & District bus was an all Kentish product with a Maidstone built Tilling-Stevens chassis and bodywork by Beadle of Dartford. KO115 was new in 1927 and carried thirty-one passengers. It is shown in the wide High Street at Tenterden, waiting to depart to Ashford. (Paynes Photo Service, Maidstone, no date.)

Another Tilling-Stevens/Beadle combination is seen on this postcard. It is a 1928 example in the East Kent fleet, working an express service to London through the village of Ospringe. (No publisher or date.)

Benjiman Redbourn commenced operating motor charabancs from the Granville Garage, Ramsgate, in 1913. Operations expanded and the firm later became Redbourn & Sons Ltd. Various trading names were used: Granville Coaches, Victoria Coaches and for the Margate based fleet, Harold Coaches. This postcard shows two Harold Coaches' Thornycroft charabancs on a church outing. The second vehicle can be identified as KL7141, new in May 1925. The Redbourn group passed to East Kent in 1935, and at that stage ran thirty-six vehicles. (No publisher or date.)

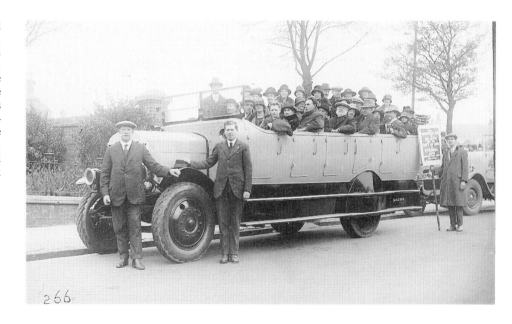

This postcard is unusual in that it is a manufacturer's advertising card. KK5410 was a Lancia with coachwork by Furber, Kentish Town, as shown on the notice by the front wheel. It was for an operator called Tatum of Herne Bay and was a type known as a gangwayed charabanc, without all the side doors. (Published by Arthur G. Furber, City Carriage Works, Crown Place, Kentish Town, NW5, in 1923.)

Alexander Timpson of Plumstead began business in 1896 with horse-bus operation in South East London, and began running motor-buses in 1912. Expansion led to depots at Ramsgate and Hastings and a network of coastal express services. The postcard shows DY1141, a Hastings registered Karrier charabanc at Westgate Road, Dartford, heading for the coast. Timpson's Hastings operations were sold to Maidstone & District in 1934, but otherwise the firm survived until the National Bus Company era, forming part of National Travel London. (No publisher or date.)

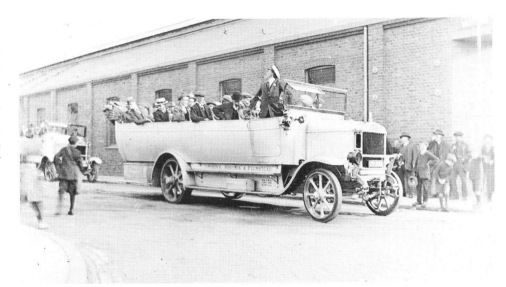

Pilchers Coaches of Chatham were the oldest established coach operators in Kent, dating back to a carrier's business begun in 1859. They ran a horse-bus service between Strood and Luton. They ceased operations in June 1984, after four generations of the family had run the business. This postcard shows KJ1563, an AEC Regal with 32-seat Duple coachwork new in 1931. It later received a second body and lasted until 1961 in the fleet! (No publisher or date.)

43

Since the demise of Pilchers Coaches, Blue Rambler Coaches, Margate, is the most likely candidate for the oldest established small operator in the area. The firm has been operating since at least the mid-twenties, when Woolf Simmonds was the proprietor. It is still run by the same family, on the female side through two generations, to this day. The coach pictured here is HS6286, a Wycombe-bodied Gilford of 1930 that ran until 1948. (No publisher, but sent from Southport to London, 2nd June 1940.)

This postcard shows Margate Harbour full of shipping, mainly Thames sailing barges and fishing boats. The same view today would have a similar number of boats, but most would be pleasure craft. (This postcard is the work of Louis Levy of Paris; compare with the earlier view of Grove Ferry without the 'LL'. Postally used locally at Blackheath, 21st July 1906.)

30   MARGATE — The Harbour from Pier. — LL

The short pier or jetty roughly opposite the station at Margate was the calling point for the coastal steamers that worked from London to Southend and on to Ramsgate or beyond. Even after the arrival of the railways there was still a heavy demand for services, as this low-tide view shows. No sooner has one boat unloaded than the next boat is coming in to berth. Note the railway line down the pier; it is not known what it was used for, but it may have been only for hand-propelled luggage carts. (Published by C. Simeons & Co. London and printed in Hessia, about 1903.)

By the 1930s sepia-tint postcards of the seaside were the staple offering of many publishers. This one is however better than the standard, as an otherwise dull view of Tankerton Slopes is enlivened by the activities of Whitstable Regatta Week. While the main yacht racing takes place in the distance, a crowd gathers on the Slopes to view the less serious activities by the locals inshore. This included rowing races and the obstacle course, with its greasy pole and other delights, which can be seen close to the beach. The sailing barge was the official's boat. (Published by West & Son, Whitstable, about 1930.)

This view of Rochester Castle and Cathdral from across the Medway has featured in many postcards over the years. This photograph has also been used as the basis of many different prints of postcards, both black & white and colour. The Thames sailing barge has just come upstream under the Rochester Bridges and the crew, assisted by a 'huffler', are busily winching the main mast back into place. In the heyday of rail there were always 'hufflers' available as extra crew with local knowledge to assist barges with the difficult job of shooting Rochester Bridge. (Published by Valentines, Dundee, and sent locally in London, 10th June 1924.)

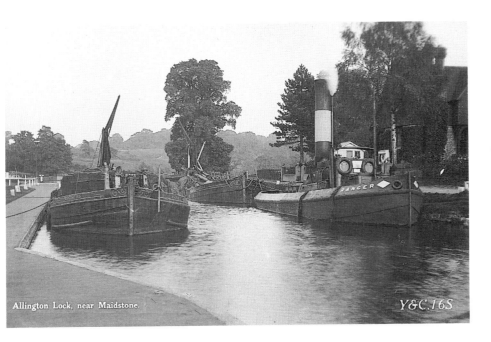

Upstream from Rochester the first lock is that at Allington, a few miles from Maidstone. This postcard shows the steam tug *Ranger* with a barge in tow heading seawards. Other barges can be seen, though the two with their masts up will not get far with Maidstone Bridge one way and Aylesford Bridge the other. (Published by Young & Cooper, Maidstone, no date.)

A Pou-de-Ciel, or flying flea, was the 1930s equivalent of the modern microlight craft. Many were involved in fatal crashes, but G-AEEB photographed at Penshurst survived and is now in the Shuttleworth Collection.

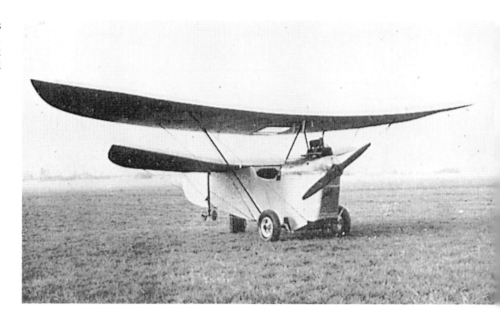

The Vickers Virginia was introduced in 1924 as the RAF's heavy bomber. This example was based at RAF Manston and is seen flying over Kent. (Postcard by Flight.)

On 16th March 1933 this Imperial Airways A.W. Argosy II inbound from Cologne and Brussels was diverted to Gravesend due to poor visibility at Croydon. It was then damaged by strong winds that night, and had to be taken away by road for repairs.

Finally a few postcards of the Medway Towns. The vast Chatham Dockyard complex provided enormous scope for the publisher, seemingly without any censorship on subject matter; in those days flag-waving was more important than secrecy. This view of a somewhat mixed reserve fleet about 1904 would not impress anyone! (Published by Gale & Polden, Aldershot, a firm which not surprisingly specialised in military subjects.)

Another postcard from the same series returns to the subject of Chatham trams. There was always a rush for the first trams after knocking-off time; apart from the desire to get home, only the first four cars gave special workmen's fares and it was full fare if one failed to get on these. As a reminder of how many men worked in the Dockyard until quite recently, on the wall on the east side of Dock Road can be seen the names of various areas of the Medway Towns. These were the stopping points for the Maidstone & District works buses. (Published by Gale & Polden, Aldershot, about 1904.)

Like the pier at Margate, the Medway was also served by a number of paddle-steamers running regular ferry services. This card shows P.S. *City of Rochester*, which plied from Strood to Southend. Such services ceased many years ago, but recently the preserved paddle-steamer P.S. *Kingswear Castle* has again operated this service. (Published by W.N. Eastgate Series, Rochester, about 1905.)

For many years Short Bros of Rochester built seaplanes at their works on Rochester Esplanade. These were often seen on the Medway, like this Shorts *Mussel*. The first example of this model was built in 1925. It was designed largely for flying clubs, and in 1928 one broke the world altitude record for float planes. (No publisher or date.)

Later Shorts built the famous Empire flying boats and in 1938 came the unique Short-Mayo composite. It consisted of *Maia*, a modified Empire flying boat and *Mercury*, a four-engined float plane. The idea was to give the float plane a greater range and load by using the power and fuel of the larger flying boat during take-off. The aim was to improve air mail carriage around the Empire and a number of successful separations were made, including one when *Mercury* flew non-stop from Scotland to South Africa, an endurance record for a float plane that is still unbroken. (Published by Medway Studios Ltd, High Street, Chatham, 1938.)

During the lean years of the 1920s, Shorts turned to other work, including bus bodywork, often for local operators. Photographs of such buses were taken on Rochester Esplanade. Maidstone & District were frequent customers, but this 1928 Tilling-Stevens has Harrington coachwork, although Shorts did build some bus-bodied examples for M&D in this year. Perhaps it was a Short Bros outing? (No publisher or date.)